Break the Code

Cryptography for Beginners

Bud Johnson

Illustrations by Larry Daste

Dover Publications, Inc.

Mineola, New York

Dedication

To my beautiful wife, Evelyne—my love, my partner, without whose insight, belief and encouragement my crypto career would not have happened.

To M/Sgt. Jimmy West,
who "awakened" me to the excitement and complexities of cryptography.

And to the loving memory of Sgt. William E. (Bill) Kelly, my Army Air Corps buddy.
From the jungles to the desert, we 'crypt' through it all—
from cryptography school to a lifelong friendship, you made it a blast, Kel.

About the Author

Bud Johnson served in World War II as a cryptographer/ cryptanalyst for the Army Air Corps. The activities of his and other overseas field intelligence units in the interception of enemy coded messages and the capture of codes and code equipment were important contributions to the successful Normandy landings of the Allied invasion forces, in June 1944, as well as to the war effort in general. In June 1994, Bud Johnson was honored by the French government with two medals for his wartime work.

Bibliographical Note

Break the Code: Cryptography for Beginners is a new work, first published by Dover Publications, Inc., in 1997.

Library of Congress Cataloging-in-Publication Data

Johnson, Bud.
   Break the code : cryptography for beginners / Bud Johnson ; illustrations by Larry Daste.
      p.   cm.
   ISBN-13: 978-0-486-29146-8
   ISBN-10: 0-486-29146-4
   1. Cryptography.   I. Title.
Z103.J65 1997
652' .8—dc21   97–19323
                                                                    CIP

Manufactured in the United States by LSC Communications
29146412   2017
www.doverpublications.com

Contents

Introduction

ENCOD INGAN DDECO
DINGA RELOT SOFFU NWXYZ

No, it's not gibberish! Read letter by letter until you find a word—
in this case, **ENCODING**. Keep going and you'll find that the coded
message reads: **Encoding and decoding are lots of fun (wxyz)**
(Those nonsense letters at the end—"wxyz"— make the message even trickier to read!)

You now know one way to decode—but can you . . .

EGASS EMDED OCEHT KAERB

It's easy. Just read the message *backwards* to **Break the coded message.**

Almost everyone is intrigued by secrets. In fact, over the centuries
many famous people—and some infamous ones, too—have used secret
methods of writing. Even today, governments, businesses and all sorts
of organizations regularly use codes to communicate.

In our book, we'll introduce you to some of the techniques used in
this mysterious global world of codes, ciphers and secret writing. You'll
learn how each technique works . . . how to break that kind of code . . .
and how to use that technique to create your own secret messages.
And you'll have plenty to solve with all the practice messages scattered
throughout these pages.   The cartoons may help you solve the secrets—
but if they don't, all of the solutions are printed at the end of the book.

Have fun! Enjoy!

"Crypto" Talk

Here are some terms commonly used by cryptographers.

BREAKING A CODE

Discovering (learning) the intricacies of the formula that someone has used to create a code unknown to you. The process of unravelling such a code can be very complex, and may require breaking scores or hundreds or even thousands of coded messages before the actual code itself can be broken.

BREAKING A MESSAGE

The act of translating a message from code to cleartext.

CLEARTEXT or IN THE CLEAR or PLAINTEXT

A message written in plain language, as opposed to a coded or enciphered message.

CODES and/or CIPHERS

These terms are sometimes used interchangeably. Technically, however, a code requires the use of a code book, or a pre-selected book or a periodical known only to the sender and the receiver; both must have the code key being used for a message. Without the code book and code key, it is impossible to break a coded message.

Ciphers are more interesting. In a cipher, each plaintext letter is changed by substituting another letter for it, or by transposing (shifting) it in some way.

To avoid unnecessary confusion in terminology, this book uses the words "code," "encoding" and "decoding" to describe selected techniques for secret writing.

CODE BOOK

A book containing words and/or symbols used in coded messages, together with their actual (plaintext) meaning.

CODE KEY

Words or symbols—sometimes *both* used in combination—to denote the type of code being used, along with one or more key elements of the code or cipher. In the "twisted path" code, for example (see pp. 58–9), a sample code key is

$$5x6V \uparrow \downarrow \downarrow \uparrow \downarrow R/L$$

—containing all of the basic information one needs to break a specific coded message.

"CRYPTO"

Slang (among fellow professionals) for "cryptographer" or "cryptanalyst."

CRYPTOGRAPHY

The art and science of creating and breaking codes and ciphers.

DECODING

The process of changing a coded message back into its original plaintext form.

ENCODING

The process of changing plaintext into code.

MONOALPHABETIC / POLYALPHABETIC

In a monoalphabetic system, one letter substitutes for one and only one letter. In a polyalphabetic system, one letter may stand in place of different letters within the same message.

GARBLE or GARBLED MESSAGE

An encoded message that has been messed up due to errors in its transmission or reception. The text may skip one or more letters, letter groups and/or whole sections of the message.

NULL(S)

A dummy or nonsense letter or group of letters inserted in a message—usually at its beginning or end. The purpose of the null is to fill out a short (incomplete) 5-letter or 4-letter group in an encoded message.

SUBSTITUTION CIPHER

A code that exchanges one plaintext letter for another.

TRANSPOSITION CIPHER

A code that changes the order or sequence of letters in the plaintext message.

Ready-made Alphabets
for Shift and Key Word Codes

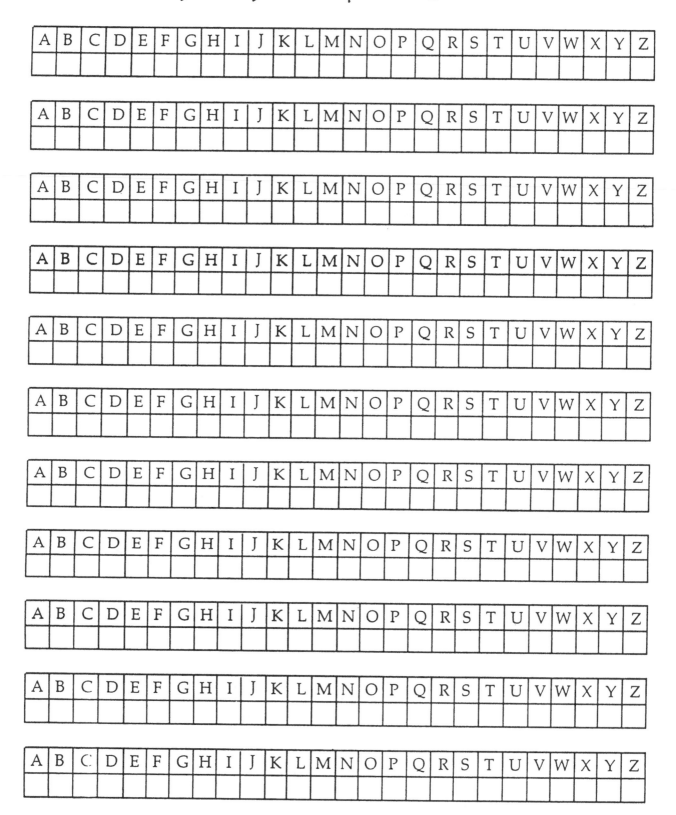

Break the Code

Cryptography for Beginners

Simple Letter Grouping

It's easy to read this sentence . . . *but* . . .

ITSEA SYTOR EADTH ISSEN TENCE

will make you stop and think because it makes no sense and looks so weird. What does it mean?

Here's how we made up this secret message:
• First, we wrote out the message "It's easy to read this sentence" in *capital* letters—but *without* any punctuation and with the words *squeezed together*:

ITSEASYTOREADTHISSENTENCE

(You have to admit that it already looks pretty mysterious!)

• Then we divided the message into *5-letter groups*, like this . . .

ITSEA SYTOR EADTH ISSEN TENCE

. . . and—*presto chango*—we created a simple secret message!

Did you know that writing in either 4-letter groups or 5-letter groups is the standard way that professional cryptographers all over the world encode their messages? It's a quick way to slow down somebody's reading speed—and it's especially puzzling for readers who have never seen this technique before. In this book, we'll stick to 5-letter groups only.

"It's easy to read this sentence" worked great because those six words divided evenly into 5-letter groups. But what will you do with *this* message?

SECRET MEETING AT ONE

Changed into code, it becomes . . .

SECRE TMEET INGAT ONE

What's wrong with it? *It's too short.* That **E** at the end needs two more letters to complete its 5-letter group.

"Nulls" to the rescue! The solution is easy if you add two "nulls" —any dummy or nonsense letters— to fill out that short 5-letter group. For instance, if you pick **QX** as your nulls, the message would read:

SECRE TMEET INGAT ONEQX

Or you can complicate the code even more by placing the nulls at the *beginning* of the secret message, just to make its meaning even harder to solve:

QXSEC RETME ETING ATONE

As soon as you break the coded messages that follow, make up some of your own to send to your fellow cryptographers.

SECRET MESSAGE NO. 1

Code: Letter grouping
Key: 5-letter groups

Coded message:

```
PATIE  NCEAN  DFORT  ITUDE  ARERE  NOWNL  ANDMA
RKSAN  DTHEM  ANEGU  ARDIA  NSATT  HEMAI  NENTR
ANCEO  FTHEN  EWYOR  KPUBL  ICLIB  RARYL  OCATE
DATFI  FTHAV  ENUEA  NDFOR  TYSEC  ONDST  REETI
NNEWY  ORKCI  TYAKA  THEBI  GAPPL  EOQBR
```

Decoded message:

Print out the complete message in capital letters, with no spaces between letters. Mark a slash (/) between words as they appear to you.

—— —— —— —— —— —— —— —— —— —— —— —— —— —— ——

—— —— —— —— —— —— —— —— —— —— —— —— —— —— ——

—— —— —— —— —— —— —— —— —— —— —— —— —— —— ——

—— —— —— —— —— —— —— —— —— —— —— —— —— —— ——

—— —— —— —— —— —— —— —— —— —— —— —— —— —— ——

—— —— —— —— —— —— —— —— —— —— —— —— —— —— ——

—— —— —— —— —— —— —— —— —— —— —— ——

Cleartext message:

Write out the complete message in plain English.

SECRET MESSAGE NO. 2

Code: Letter grouping
Key: 5-letter groups

Coded message:

THELO NEEAG LECHA RLESA UGUST USLIN DBERG
HFLEW THESP IRITO FSTLO UISON HISHI STORI
CFLIG HTWHI CHINR ETROS PECTC ANBEL IKENE
DTOTH EPLAC INGOF THEFI RSTSP ANOFT HENOW
MUCHT RAVEL EDAIR BRIDG ERWMB

Decoded message:

Print out the complete message in capital letters, with no spaces between
letters. Mark a slash (/) between words as they appear to you.

_____

_____

_____

_____

_____

_____

_____

Cleartext message:

Write out the complete message in plain English.

5

SECRET MESSAGE NO. 3

Code: Letter grouping
Key: 5-letter groups

Coded message:

THEPR OFUSI ONOFP RODUC TSREL ATEDT OTHEI
NVENT IVEGE NIUSO FTHOM ASALV AEDIS ONTOU
CHTHE LIVES OFTHE MAJOR ITYOF THEPO PULAT
IONSP ANNIN GTHEG LOBEC ONTRI BUTIN GTOTH
EIRCO MFORT ANDWE LLBEI NGBCR

Decoded message:

Print out the complete message in capital letters, with no spaces between letters. Mark a slash (/) between words as they appear to you.

_ _

_ _

_ _

_ _

_ _

_ _ _ _ _ _ _ _ _ _ _ _ _ _ _ _ _ _

_ _ _ _ _ _ _ _ _ _ _ _ _ _ _

Cleartext message:

Write out the complete message in plain English.

6

SECRET MESSAGE NO. 4

Code: Letter grouping
Key: 5-letter groups

Coded message:

EXHIB ITING RAREF ORESI GHTBL ESSED WITHO
RATOR ICALM AGNIF ICENC EANDP OSSES SINGA
SPIRA TIONS ANDDR EAMSB EYOND COMPA REDRM
ARTIN LUTHE RKING JRWAS ASING ULARG IANTW
ITHTH EPOWE ROFOU TSTAN DINGL EADER SHIPQ

[Suggestion: If one of your own secret messages turns up obvious or nearly recognizable words—like **ARTIN LUTHE RKING** in the message above—try placing any nulls at the *beginning* instead of at the end. This will help complicate the look of the coded message.]

Decoded message:

Print out the complete message in capital letters, with no spaces between letters. Mark a slash (/) between words as they appear to you.

_ _

_ _

_ _

_ _

_ _

_ _

_ _ _ _ _ _ _ _ _ _ _ _ _ _ _ _ _ _ _ _ _ _ _ _ _ _

Cleartext message:

Write out the complete message in plain English.

7

SECRET MESSAGE No. 5

Code: Letter grouping
Key: 5-letter groups

Coded message:

CREAT ORAND CONDU CTORO FTHEU NDERG ROUND
RAILR OADTH EASTO NISHI NGINN OVATO RHARR
IETTU BMANT HOUGH BORNA SLAVE HELDF ORTHA
FREES PIRIT EXHIB ITEDF EATSO FREMA RKABL
EHERO ISMAN DBECA MEANI NSPIR ATION TOPEO
PLESO FTHEF REEWO RLDTZ

Decoded message:

Print out the complete message in capital letters, with no spaces between letters. Mark a slash (/) between words as they appear to you.

——————————————————————————————————

——————————————————————————————————

——————————————————————————————————

——————————————————————————————————

——————————————————————————————————

——————————————————————————————————

——————————————————————————————————

————————————————————————————

Cleartext message:

Write out the complete message in plain English.

SECRET MESSAGE No. 6

Code: Letter grouping
Key: 5-letter groups

Coded message:

RECOG NIZED FORHE RDIST INGUI SHEDC AREER
ASANA SSIST ANTAT TORNE YGENE RALST ATESE
NATOR ANDAS UPERI ORCOU RTJUD GESAN DRADA
YOCON NORBO RNINE LPASO TXWAS THEFI RSTWO
MANAP POINT EDTOS ERVEA SANAS SOCIA TEJUS
TICEO FTHEU SSUPR EMECO URTMZ

[In the fourth line, notice how the abbreviation **TX** avoids spelling out "TEXAS"
as a complete, and obvious, 5-letter group. In your own dispatches, use common
abbreviations wherever possible to help confuse the look of your secret message.]

Decoded message:

Print out the complete message in capital letters, with no spaces between
letters. Mark a slash (/) between words as they appear to you.

_ _

_ _

_ _

_ _

_ _

_ _

_ _

_ _

Cleartext message:

Write out the complete message in plain English.

9

SECRET MESSAGE NO. 7

Code: Letter grouping
Key: 5-letter groups

Coded message:

NOTAB LEAMO NGAME RICAN JURIS TSRUT HBADE
RGINS BERGB ORNIN BROOK LYNNY ISTHE SECON
DWOMA NAPPO INTED TOTHE SUPRE MECOU RTAPR
OFESS OROFL AWSHE GAINE DWIDE RECOG NITIO
NANDW ASNOT EDFOR HERAC COMPL ISHME NTSTO
WARDH ELPIN GTOEN DINST ITUTI ONALI ZEDDI
SCRIM INATI ONAGA INSTW OMENX

Decoded message:

— —

— —

— —

— —

— —

— —

— —

— —

— — — — — — — — — — — —

Cleartext message:

10

SECRET MESSAGE NO. 8

Code: Letter grouping
Key: 5-letter groups

Coded message:

PTRPN URTUR INGTH ETHEO RYOFR ELATI VITYA
LBERT EINST EINBE CAMEA NOBEL LAURE ATEFO
RHISW ORKIN PHYSI CSALT HOUGH SOMEO FHISC
ONCEP TSAND THEOR IESDI DNOTG AINUN IVERS
ALACC EPTAN CEHIS SCIEN TIFIC ANDSO CIALE
FFORT SANDF REETH INKIN GGAIN EDHIM WORLD
WIDER ECOGN ITION

Decoded message:

_ _

_ _

_ _

_ _

_ _

_ _

_ _

_ _

_ _

Cleartext message:

11

The Reverse Trail

We know that you've already read this sentence . . . *but* . . .

**ECNET NESSI HTDAE RYDAE
RLAEV UOYTA HTWON KEWQX**

will stop everybody in their tracks because it looks like complete nonsense. What does it mean? (Read it backwards! The **X** and **Q** are nulls.)

Here's how we made up this secret message:

• First, we wrote out the message . . .

"We know that you've already read this sentence"

. . . in *capital* letters, but without any punctuation:

WE KNOW THAT YOUVE ALREADY READ THIS SENTENCE

• Then we wrote it out *backwards,* with the words *squeezed together:*

ECNETNESSIHTDAERYDAERLAEVUOYTAHTWONKEW

(Do you suppose an interceptor will try to *pronounce* it?!)

• Then, as we did before, we *divided* the message into *5-letter groups,* like this . . .

**ECNET NESSI HTDAE RYDAE
RLAEV UOYTA HTWON KEWQX**

. . . adding the nulls **QX** to fill out the last 5-letter group.

A "reverse trail" code may seem easy to break, but you can fool even the smartest "spy" by the way you choose your words.

Suppose you wanted to tell your buddy that your secret meeting planned for 11 a.m. has to take place at 9 a.m. Instead of writing the obvious message, you could say:

WE HAVE TO DWARF [shorten] THE TIME. ELEVEN HUNDRED SHRINKS [goes back] TO ZERO NINE OH OH.

(Notice that we're using military talk to disguise 11 a.m.—"1100 hours"—and 9 a.m.—"0900 hours.")

Then, encoding this message as a "reverse trail," you would write:

HOHOE NINOR EZOTS KNIRH SDERD NUHNE
VELEE MITEH TFRAW DOTEV AHEWR

(The last **R** is a null.)

Here's a real opportunity for your imagination and innovation. But don't outsmart yourself! Be clever and crafty, but be certain that your message will be understood. *Clarity* is essential in preparing a message. *Patience, common sense* and *careful preparation* are essential when it comes time to encode it. To simplify the job, you may want to handprint your message on a copy of the grid paper supplied near the front of the book. Use one box for each capital letter.

As soon as you break the encoded "reverse trail" messages that follow, create some of your own to send to your fellow cryptographers.

SECRET MESSAGE NO. 9

Code: Reverse trail
Key: 5-letter groups

Coded message:

SEOEG NIHTO NROFS KNAHT

Decoded message:

- Going *in reverse*—from right to left—print out each capital letter, one after the other, until you reach the beginning of the secret message.
- Don't leave any spaces between letters.
- Mark a slash (/) between words as they appear to you.

— — — — — — — — — — — — — — — — — — —

Cleartext message:

Write out the complete message in plain English.

14

Code: Reverse trail
Key: 5-letter groups

Coded message:

> VRQMT URANI KCUTS TEGUO YEROF
> EBKCI UQEBK CAJEL BMINE BKCAJ

Decoded message:

- Going *in reverse*—from right to left—print out each capital letter, one after the other, until you reach the beginning of the secret message.
- Don't leave any spaces between letters.
- Mark a slash (/) between words as they appear to you.

— — — — — — — — — — — — — — — — — — — —

— — — — — — — — — — — — — — — — — — —

— — — — — — — — —

Cleartext message:

Write out the complete message in plain English.

SECRET MESSAGE No. 11

Code: Reverse trail
Key: 5-letter groups

Coded message:

LLEWS   DNETA   HTLLE   WSLLA

Decoded message:

- Going *in reverse*—from right to left—print out each capital letter, one after the other, until you reach the beginning of the secret message.
- Don't leave any spaces between letters.
- Mark a slash (/) between words as they appear to you.

- -

Cleartext message:

Write out the complete message in plain English.

Code: Reverse trail
Key: 5-letter groups

Coded message:

**TRTMT SRIFE BLLAH STSAL EHTDN
ATSAL EBLLA HSTSR IFEHT**

Decoded message:

Remember to *reverse* the message with no spaces between letters—
and mark a slash between words as they appear to you.

_ _

_ _

_ _ _ _ _ _ _ _ _ _ _

Cleartext message:

Write out the complete message in plain English.

SECRET MESSAGE NO. 13

Code: Reverse trail
Key: 5-letter groups

Coded message:

WMSEN   IHSNU   SEHTE   LIHWY   AHEKA   MSTEL

Decoded message:

Remember to *reverse* the message with no spaces between letters—
and mark a slash between words as they appear to you.

— — — — — — — — — — — — — — — —

— — — — — — — — — — — — — — — —

Cleartext message:

Write out the complete message in plain English.

SECRET MESSAGE No. 14

Code: Reverse trail
Key: 5-letter groups

Coded message:

**VRHSU BEHTN IOWTH
TROWS IDNAH EHTNI DRIBA**

Decoded message:

_ _ _ _ _ _ _ _ _ _ _ _ _ _ _ _ _

_ _ _ _ _ _ _ _ _ _ _ _ _ _ _ _ _ _

Cleartext message:

SECRET MESSAGE NO. 15

Code: Reverse trail
Key: 5-letter groups

Coded message:

OGNIH TDOOG AFOHC
UMOOT EVAHR EVENN ACUOY

Decoded message:

— — — — — — — — — — — — — —

— — — — — — — — — — — — — — —

Cleartext message:

SECRET MESSAGE NO. 16

Code: Reverse trail
Key: 5-letter groups

Coded message:

OXRLL   ATADA   ERBON   NAHTF
AOLAF   LAHAR   ETTEB

Decoded message:

BETTERAHALFALOAFTHANNOBREADATALL RXO

Cleartext message:

BETTER A HALF A LOAF THAN NO BREAD AT ALL

21

Shift Code

A "shift code" uses TWO alphabets, one on top of the other.

The *upper* alphabet is called the PLAINTEXT alphabet.
It shows your message in <u>plain English</u>.

PLAINTEXT	A	B	C	D	E	F	G	H	I	J	K	L	M	N	O	P	Q	R	S	T	U	V	W	X	Y	Z
SHIFT	A	B	C	D	E	F	G	H	I	J	K	L	M	N	O	P	Q	R	S	T	U	V	W	X	Y	Z

The *lower* alphabet is called the **SHIFT** alphabet
because it's going to slide (shift) all over the place!
It will show your secret message in <u>code</u> (as soon as we shift it!).

Now let's slide the **SHIFT** alphabet <u>one place to the right</u>
so that letter "**A**" falls right under PLAINTEXT letter "B."
Call this a **"SHIFT + 1"** code (to describe that 1-space slide):

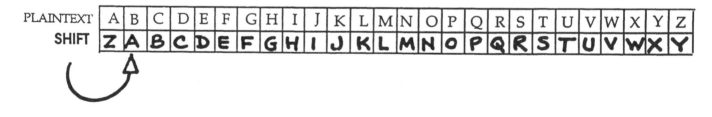

PLAINTEXT	A	B	C	D	E	F	G	H	I	J	K	L	M	N	O	P	Q	R	S	T	U	V	W	X	Y	Z
SHIFT	Z	A	B	C	D	E	F	G	H	I	J	K	L	M	N	O	P	Q	R	S	T	U	V	W	X	Y

This time let's slide the **SHIFT** alphabet <u>three places to the right</u>
so that letter "**A**" now falls right under PLAINTEXT letter "D."
Call this a **"SHIFT + 3"** code (to describe that 3-space slide):

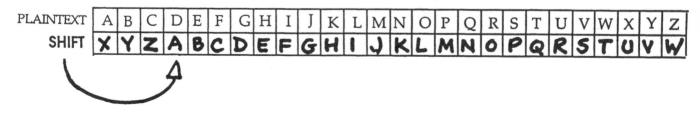

PLAINTEXT	A	B	C	D	E	F	G	H	I	J	K	L	M	N	O	P	Q	R	S	T	U	V	W	X	Y	Z
SHIFT	X	Y	Z	A	B	C	D	E	F	G	H	I	J	K	L	M	N	O	P	Q	R	S	T	U	V	W

For starters, let's decode the secret message below using the **SHIFT + 3** code.

IBQQE BDXJB PYBDF KWLON

STEP 1:   Write out both alphabets, moving the **SHIFT** alphabet **3** places to the right.

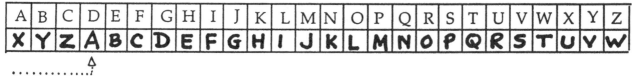

STEP 2:   Letter by letter, look up the coded message in the **SHIFT** alphabet: I...B...Q... and so on. Then *substitute* each of those letters with its corresponding letter in the PLAINTEXT alphabet:

(The substitute for I is L... The substitute for B is E... The substitute for Q is T...)

$$I = L$$
$$B = E$$
$$Q = T$$
$$Q = T$$
$$E = H$$

STEP 3:   As soon as you've found all the substitutes, write out your complete PLAINTEXT message (still in 5-letter groups):

L E T T H   E G A M E   S B E G I   N Z O R Q

STEP 4:   Finally, use common sense and logic to find one good word after the other in the PLAINTEXT message, until you have the complete message in plain English. A plain English message is called a "cleartext" message, or a message that's "in the clear."

This one says:

"ZORQ" are nulls

LET THE GAMES BEGIN ZORQ

SECRET MESSAGE NO. 17

Code: Shift code
Key: SHIFT + 3

Coded message:

ALKQD FSBRM QEBPE FMZDO

Composition for decoding:

- Print the **SHIFT + 3** alphabet below this PLAINTEXT alphabet.

A	B	C	D	E	F	G	H	I	J	K	L	M	N	O	P	Q	R	S	T	U	V	W	X	Y	Z

Plaintext message:

- Letter by letter, look up the coded message in the SHIFT (lower) alphabet.
- Then substitute each of those letters with its corresponding letter in the PLAINTEXT (upper) alphabet.
- Print the complete plaintext message in 5-letter groups.

_____ _____ _____ _____

Cleartext message:

- Use slashes (/) to divide the plaintext message into recognizable words.
- Write out the complete message in plain English.

24

SECRET MESSAGE NO. 18

Code: Shift code
Key: SHIFT + 8

Coded message:

VGFLK   OWSLE   WRBPZ

Composition for decoding:

- Print the **SHIFT + 8** alphabet below this PLAINTEXT alphabet.

A	B	C	D	E	F	G	H	I	J	K	L	M	N	O	P	Q	R	S	T	U	V	W	X	Y	Z

Plaintext message:

- Letter by letter, look up the coded message in the SHIFT (lower) alphabet.
- Then substitute each of those letters with its corresponding letter in the PLAINTEXT (upper) alphabet.
- Print the complete plaintext message in 5-letter groups.

—————   —————   —————

Cleartext message:

- Use slashes (/) to divide the plaintext message into recognizable words.
- Write out the complete message in plain English.

25

SECRET MESSAGE NO. 19

Code: Shift code
Key: SHIFT + 2

Coded message:

GRQYQ NJYGL YQRFC LMQCM LWMSP DYACV

Composition for decoding:

- Print the **SHIFT + 2** alphabet below this PLAINTEXT alphabet.

A	B	C	D	E	F	G	H	I	J	K	L	M	N	O	P	Q	R	S	T	U	V	W	X	Y	Z

Plaintext message:

- Letter by letter, look up the coded message in the SHIFT (lower) alphabet.
- Then substitute each of those letters with its corresponding letter in the PLAINTEXT (upper) alphabet.
- Print the complete plaintext message in 5-letter groups.

_ _ _ _ _   _ _ _ _ _   _ _ _ _ _

_ _ _ _ _   _ _ _ _ _   _ _ _ _ _

Cleartext message:

- Use slashes (/) to divide the plaintext message into recognizable words.
- Write out the complete message in plain English.

26

SECRET MESSAGE NO. 20

Code: Shift code
Key: SHIFT + 4

Coded message:

WJEHH SEJZX HKSOJ KCKKZ

Composition for decoding:

- Print the **SHIFT + 4** alphabet below this PLAINTEXT alphabet.

A	B	C	D	E	F	G	H	I	J	K	L	M	N	O	P	Q	R	S	T	U	V	W	X	Y	Z

Plaintext message:

- As you've already learned to do, substitute a PLAINTEXT letter for each letter in the secret message.

————   ————   ————   ————

Cleartext message:

- What does the coded message say?

Code: Shift code
Key: SHIFT + 6

Coded message:

XIHNF   IIEUA   CZNBI   LMYCH   NBYGI   ONBRS

Composition for decoding:

- Print the **SHIFT + 6** alphabet below this PLAINTEXT alphabet.

A	B	C	D	E	F	G	H	I	J	K	L	M	N	O	P	Q	R	S	T	U	V	W	X	Y	Z

Plaintext message:

- As you've already learned to do, substitute a PLAINTEXT letter for each letter in the secret message.

_ _ _ _ _   _ _ _ _ _   _ _ _ _ _

_ _ _ _ _   _ _ _ _ _   _ _ _ _ _

Cleartext message:

- What does the coded message say?

SECRET MESSAGE NO. 22

Code: Shift code
Key: SHIFT + 5

Coded message:

BZOOD IBVIV DNVWM ZZUZY VNCIJ OLSML

Composition for decoding:

A	B	C	D	E	F	G	H	I	J	K	L	M	N	O	P	Q	R	S	T	U	V	W	X	Y	Z

Plaintext message:

───── ───── ─────

───── ───── ─────

Cleartext message:

29

SECRET MESSAGE NO. 23

Code: Shift code
Key: SHIFT + 5

Coded message:

KMJIO JJCOR JCPIY MZYOC
ZMVDY CDONV NKGVI IZYLU

Composition for decoding:

A	B	C	D	E	F	G	H	I	J	K	L	M	N	O	P	Q	R	S	T	U	V	W	X	Y	Z

Plaintext message:

_ _ _ _ _   _ _ _ _ _   _ _ _ _ _   _ _ _ _ _

_ _ _ _ _   _ _ _ _ _   _ _ _ _ _   _ _ _ _ _

Cleartext message:

30

SECRET MESSAGE NO. 24

Code: Shift code
Key: SHIFT + 14

Coded message:

LUXOT BDASD QEEEO DMFOT FTQBA IIAIJ

Composition for decoding:

A	B	C	D	E	F	G	H	I	J	K	L	M	N	O	P	Q	R	S	T	U	V	W	X	Y	Z

Plaintext message:

_ _ _ _ _   _ _ _ _ _   _ _ _ _ _

_ _ _ _ _   _ _ _ _ _   _ _ _ _ _

Cleartext message:

31

SECRET MESSAGE NO. 25

Code: Shift code
Key: SHIFT + 7

Coded message:

UNLRT LTUXT OXKLE RTLTY HQPBL
XTLTG HPEUN MPAHZ BOXLT AHHMU

Composition for decoding:

A	B	C	D	E	F	G	H	I	J	K	L	M	N	O	P	Q	R	S	T	U	V	W	X	Y	Z

Plaintext message:

BUSYA SABEA VERSL YASAF OXWIS

EASAN OWLBU TWHOG IVESA HOOTB

Cleartext message:

32

Make Your Own Secret Message

It's quick and easy to <u>en</u>code your own message. Just *reverse* the steps you followed to <u>de</u>code somebody else's message!

- Think up a good message to send to a fellow codebreaker. It could be something like . . .

WATCH CHANNEL TWO AT SIX

- Then write out the double alphabet of your chosen **SHIFT CODE.***
  Let's suppose you pick **SHIFT + 5:**

PLAINTEXT	A	B	C	D	E	F	G	H	I	J	K	L	M	N	O	P	Q	R	S	T	U	V	W	X	Y	Z
SHIFT	V	W	X	Y	Z	A	B	C	D	E	F	G	H	I	J	K	L	M	N	O	P	Q	R	S	T	U

- Now use these substitution alphabets to encode your message.
  √ Find your message, letter by letter, in the PLAINTEXT alphabet.
  √ For each letter—W-A-T-C-H (etc.)— substitute its corresponding letter in the **SHIFT** alphabet:

W = **R**
A = **V**
T = **O**
C = **X**   (and so on)

- When you're done, break up your secret message into 5-letter groups . . .

RVOXC XCVII ZGORJ VONDS   (no nulls this time)

. . . and send it to your fellow codebreaker with the code key **SHIFT + 5** or **SP5** (**P** stands for "plus") or whatever secret symbol you like best . . . and tell him or her to send you an answer to decode!

---

*Extra alphabet blanks are printed on the back of the blank grid paper near the front of this book. You can photocopy both sides of that sheet for all future codemaking and codebreaking!

Key Word Code

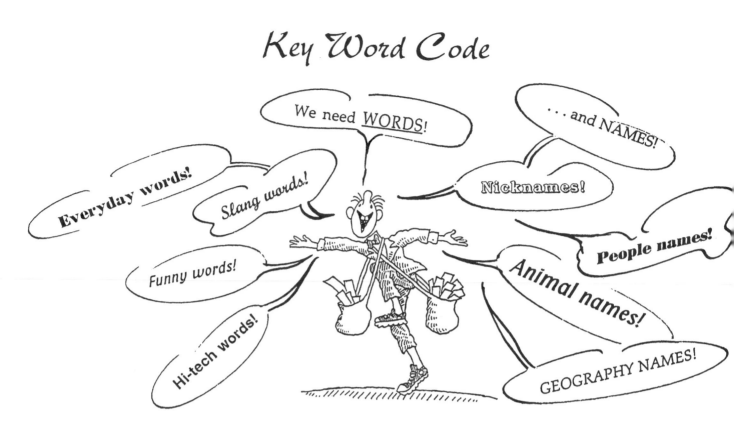

We need <u>WORDS</u>!

... and NAMES!

Everyday words!

Slang words!

Nicknames!

Funny words!

People names!

Animal names!

Hi-tech words!

GEOGRAPHY NAMES!

BUT *NO* WORDS OR NAMES WITH *DUPLICATE* LETTERS
like **BOSTON** (two O's) . . . or **ANNIE** (two N's) . . . or **DAYDREAM** (two D's and two A's)
(They don't work in Key Word codes.)

STEP 1

Look familiar? It's the same PLAINTEXT alphabet you already know:

A	B	C	D	E	F	G	H	I	J	K	L	M	N	O	P	Q	R	S	T	U	V	W	X	Y	Z

But this time there's no sliding "shift" alphabet underneath it.

STEP 2

This time, those empty boxes are waiting for a "key word"—
that secret *word* or secret *name* you've picked out.

Here's a sample, with the key word **FUNTIME** beginning the bottom
alphabet:

A	B	C	D	E	F	G	H	I	J	K	L	M	N	O	P	Q	R	S	T	U	V	W	X	Y	Z
F	U	N	T	I	M	E																			

Now comes the mystery!

What happens next will make your code so confusing that nobody—
nobody!—except your fellow cryptographer will ever figure out your secret
message.

STEP 3

FILL IN THE EMPTY BOXES WITH ALPHABET LETTERS <u>YOU HAVEN'T USED!</u>

A	B	C	D	E	F	G	H	I	J	K	L	M	N	O	P	Q	R	S	T	U	V	W	X	Y	Z
F	U	N	T	I	M	E	A	B	C	D	G	H	J	K	L	O	P	Q	R	S	V	W	X	Y	Z

- Notice that the bottom alphabet *skips* letters that are already "used up"
  by the key word.
- There's no **E** or **F** after **A-B-C-D** because **E** and **F** have already been used
  in the keyword **FUNTIME.**
- The bottom alphabet also skips past **I, M, N, T** and **U** for the same reason.

Can you decipher the **FUNTIME** code to name this familiar object?

- Letter by letter, look up the coded message in the **KEY CODE**
  alphabet: **F . . . R . . .** (and so on).

- Then *substitute* each of those letters with its corresponding
  letter in the PLAINTEXT alphabet:

  F = A
     R = T   (and so on)

Solve this little mystery, then tackle the unsolved puzzles
that lie ahead!

35

SECRET MESSAGE No. 26

Code: Key Word code
Key: **NEW YORK**

Coded message:

YIHQQ MONYI HGOEC

Composition for decoding:

- Print the KEY WORD below this PLAINTEXT alphabet.
  (This time only, it's a gift from your fellow "crypto"!)
- Now fill in the empty boxes with alphabet letters that haven't been
  "used up" by the KEY WORD.

A	B	C	D	E	F	G	H	I	J	K	L	M	N	O	P	Q	R	S	T	U	V	W	X	Y	Z
N	E	W	Y	O	R	K																			

Plaintext message:

- Letter by letter, look up the coded message in the KEY WORD (lower) alphabet.
- Then substitute each of those letters with its corresponding letter in the
  PLAINTEXT (upper) alphabet.
- Print the complete plaintext message in 5-letter groups.

_ _ _ _ _   _ _ _ _ _   _ _ _ _ _

Cleartext message:

- Use slashes (/) to divide the plaintext message into recognizable words.
- Write out the complete message in plain English.

Code: Key Word code
Key: **TINY MOUSE**

Coded message:

BMMHG FKGNB EFJWX

Composition for decoding:

- Print the KEY WORD below this PLAINTEXT alphabet.
  [Reminder: Always print a "key word" as an *unbroken* string
  of letters: TINY MOUSE = TINYMOUSE]
- Then fill in the empty boxes with alphabet letters that haven't
  been "used up" by the KEY WORD.

A	B	C	D	E	F	G	H	I	J	K	L	M	N	O	P	Q	R	S	T	U	V	W	X	Y	Z

Plaintext message:

- Letter by letter, look up the coded message in the KEY WORD alphabet.
- Then substitute each of those letters with its corresponding letter in the
  PLAINTEXT alphabet.
- Print the complete plaintext message in 5-letter groups.

_ _ _ _ _   _ _ _ _ _   _ _ _ _ _

Cleartext message:

- Use slashes (/) to divide the plaintext message into recognizable words.
- Write out the complete message in plain English.

SECRET MESSAGE NO. 28

Code: Key Word code
Key: **FLOWCHART**

Coded message:

VRCIT   INJGC   WJFPQ   RCNJG   FIPWJ

Composition for decoding:

- Print the KEY WORD and the rest of the alphabet.

A	B	C	D	E	F	G	H	I	J	K	L	M	N	O	P	Q	R	S	T	U	V	W	X	Y	Z

Plaintext message:

- As usual, substitute a PLAINTEXT letter for each letter in the secret message.

        — — — — —   — — — — —   — — — — —

        — — — — —   — — — — —

Cleartext message:

- What does the coded message say?

38

SECRET MESSAGE NO. 29

Code: Key Word code
Key: **SEAPORT**

Coded message:

OSNYP JONCQ FOOKQ JQBOE SNCAN

Composition for decoding:

- Print the KEY WORD and the rest of the alphabet.

A	B	C	D	E	F	G	H	I	J	K	L	M	N	O	P	Q	R	S	T	U	V	W	X	Y	Z

Plaintext message:

- As usual, substitute a PLAINTEXT letter for each letter in the secret message.

    _ _ _ _ _   _ _ _ _ _   _ _ _ _ _

    _ _ _ _ _   _ _ _ _ _

Cleartext message:

- What does the coded message say?

39

Code: Key Word code
Key: **NEWPORT**

Coded message:

RNGBF BNLBQ YELOO PMWIH QOGJQ

Composition for decoding:

A	B	C	D	E	F	G	H	I	J	K	L	M	N	O	P	Q	R	S	T	U	V	W	X	Y	Z

Plaintext message:

_ _ _ _ _   _ _ _ _ _   _ _ _ _ _

_ _ _ _ _   _ _ _ _ _

Cleartext message:

SECRET MESSAGE NO. 31

Code: Key Word code
Key: **COUNTER DISPLAY**

Coded message:

BYTRB BNKMH YNTJT HQTJC YBKDT HAWZQ

Composition for decoding:

A	B	C	D	E	F	G	H	I	J	K	L	M	N	O	P	Q	R	S	T	U	V	W	X	Y	Z

Plaintext message:

_ _ _ _ _   _ _ _ _ _   _ _ _ _ _

_ _ _ _ _   _ _ _ _ _   _ _ _ _ _

Cleartext message:

41

SECRET MESSAGE NO. 32

Code: Key Word code
Key: **ZEBRA**

Coded message:

RMAQZ XZLIA ARMMR
JARZL RXAZS ZPGLI XRGLI

Composition for decoding:

A	B	C	D	E	F	G	H	I	J	K	L	M	N	O	P	Q	R	S	T	U	V	W	X	Y	Z

Plaintext message:

_____ _____ _____

_____ _____ _____ _____

Cleartext message:

42

SECRET MESSAGE NO. 33

Code: Key Word code
Key: **COURTESY**

Coded message:

**GAHIL GAMNC DTMGC SAUCF FXGPF NAJFX
NIOTU IGTGC BILGA MNCDT MUEAF**

Composition for decoding:

A	B	C	D	E	F	G	H	I	J	K	L	M	N	O	P	Q	R	S	T	U	V	W	X	Y	Z

Plaintext message:

_____ _____ _____ _____

_____ _____ _____ _____

_____ _____ _____

Cleartext message:

43

SECRET MESSAGE NO. 34

Code: Key Word code
Key: **EASTON**

Coded message:

QSPUA RCOID

QQDKJ POBPK

ULRCO RPKKL

QXBTI

Composition for decoding:

A	B	C	D	E	F	G	H	I	J	K	L	M	N	O	P	Q	R	S	T	U	V	W	X	Y	Z

Plaintext message:

_ _ _ _ _   _ _ _ _ _

_ _ _ _ _   _ _ _ _ _

_ _ _ _ _   _ _ _ _ _

_ _ _ _ _

Cleartext message:

44

Make Your Own Secret Message

Try this one for air-tight security in codemaking! It's so secret that it's virtually impossible for anyone to break your secret code.

To make it work, you and your friend pick two or three favorite magazines or books. EACH OF YOU MUST HAVE A COPY.

Let's say you both own
(a) *Sports Illustrated* (Sept. 1996 issue) = code name: **SI996**
(b) *Reader's Digest* (July 1997 issue) = code name: **RD797**

If you're the sender, pick **any** word on **any** page for your "key word."

At the top of your coded message, let your friend know *exactly* where you got your "key word."

If you write **RD797/33-7-4**, here's what your friend will know:

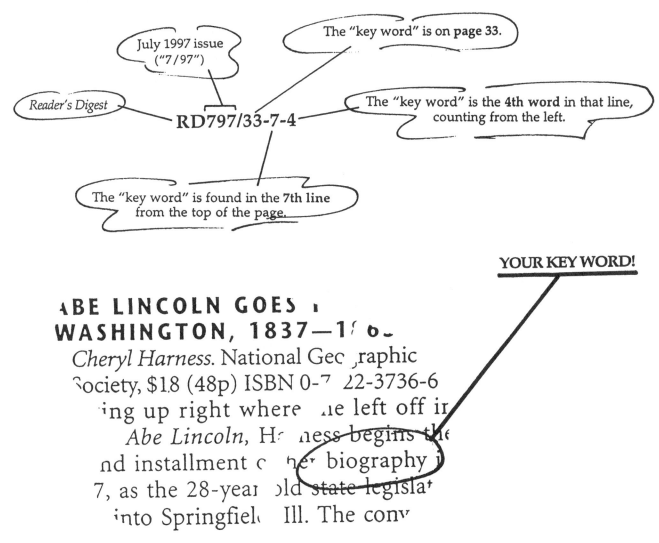

YOUR KEY WORD!

ABE LINCOLN GOES ᵗ
WASHINGTON, 1837—1⸍ ᵦ.
Cheryl Harness. National Geꞔraphic
ᵗociety, $18 (48p) ISBN 0-7 ⸝2-3736-6
ᵗng up right where ⸍ᵉ left off iᵣ
     Abe Lincoln, Hᵣ ᵣess begins tᵗᵉ
nd installment cᵗ ᵗᵉʳ biography ⸍
7, as the 28-yeaᵣ ⸍ld state legislaᵗ
ᵗnto Springfiel⸍ Ill. The conⱽ

45

Date Shift Code

Numbers???

Are you ready for a brain twister?

This one can be lots of fun—
BUT you have to <u>really</u> stay awake
along every step of doing
the fantastic **date shift** code.

Its all about *numbers*.

- "Date shift" codes always use numbers.

- The numbers can be *made up* any way you like—like **48576** . . .

- . . . or they can be based on a specific *date* as the code key.
For instance, the date <u>November 20, 1986</u> (11/20/86) would be written:
112086 . . . and <u>January 6, 1997</u> (1/6/97) would be written: **010697**.

- *But random number or specific date, be sure that both you and your fellow cryptographer know that number! Otherwise—total confusion!!!*

On the next page, we'll work out a secret message using the "date shift" code. What's astonishing—and totally different than all the other codes you know—is that *the <u>same</u> letter in your original message* . . . like the five E's in

SECRET MEETING AT FIVE
↑   ↑   ↑↑   ↑

. . . *will probably change to five <u>different</u> letters in the encoded message!*

That's why this code is called "<u>poly</u>alphabetic" ("<u>many</u> alphabets").
The other codes you know are called "<u>mono</u>alphabetic" ("<u>one</u> alphabet")

*What's "polyalphabetic"?
Never heard of it!!!*

Let's break this code! **UJIVR YBEOG NKYGR FRYFX**

Our code key is: December 3, 1996 ("12/3/96"), written **120396**

STEP ONE: Write out the encoded message.   Give it lots of room!
Write the code numbers *under* the message—**one number
for each letter**—with a little "minus" sign ("–") next to it.
When you run out of numbers, start over again.

U J I V R   Y B E O G   N K Y G R   F R Y F X
-1 -2 -0 -3 -9   -6 -1 -2 -0 -3   -9 -6 -1 -2 -0   -3 -9 -6 -1 -

STEP TWO: Print a plaintext alphabet on a work sheet. We'll refer to it
constantly to save time and avoid confusion!

A B C D E F G H I J K L M N O P Q R S T U V W X Y Z

STEP THREE: • Look at the **first** letter of the encoded message.
It is a **U** with a "–1" underneath it.
In the plaintext alphabet, what is "U" minus <u>one</u> letter ?
It is "T." **T is the first letter of the plaintext message.**

• Look at the **second** letter of the encoded message.
It is a **J** with a "–2" underneath it.
In the plaintext alphabet, what is "J" minus <u>two</u> letters ?
It is "H." **H is the second letter of the plaintext message.**

• Look at the **third** letter of the encoded message.
It is an **I** with a "–O" underneath it.
In the plaintext alphabet, what is "I" minus <u>no</u> letters ?
It is still "I." **I is the third letter of the plaintext message.**

• Look at the **fourth** letter of the encoded message.
It is a **V** with a "–3" underneath it.
In the plaintext alphabet, what is "V" minus <u>three</u> letters ?
It is "S." **S is the fourth letter of the plaintext message.**

STEP FOUR: Finally, use common sense and logic to find one good word
after the other until you have the complete message in plain
English. This one says:

THIS IS A CODE EXERCISE X

(The final"X" is a null.)

Code: Date Shift code

Key: JANUARY 20, 1994 / written **012094**

Coded message:

- Print out the following secret message on a piece of grid paper, one letter per square.
- Then print out the key number **012094** under this message— one number under each letter—with a "minus" sign ("–") in front of each number. When you run out of numbers, start over again.

AMNRX EDTNE JHTPT OVIBV VWQIR

FFOCL EZIOO VONVH NVEAY

Decoding process:

- Compare each letter of the numbered message with the plaintext alphabet below. Beginning with the first letter . . .

A minus 0 ("nothing") = A
M minus 1 = L
N minus 2 = L
R minus 0 = ??? (etc.)

A B C D E F G H I J K L M N O P Q R S T U V W X Y Z

Plaintext message:

- Write out the complete plaintext message. Use slashes (/) to divide the plaintext message into recognizable words.

————— ————— ————— ————— —————

————— ————— ————— —————

Cleartext message:

- Finally, write out the complete message in plain English.

48

SECRET MESSAGE No. 36

Code: Date Shift code
Key: AUGUST 29, 1944 / written **082944**

Coded message:

- As before, print out the secret message on a piece of grid paper.
- Then print out the key number **082944** under this message
  with a "minus" sign ("–") in front of each number.
  When you run out of numbers, start over again.

IKCVI MSIYR GSNYW NVIDD

Decoding process:

- Compare each letter of the numbered message with the plaintext
  alphabet below. Beginning with the first letter . . .

  I   minus 0 ("nothing") = I
  K   minus 8 = C (etc., etc.)

A B C D E F G H I J K L M N O P Q R S T U V W X Y Z

Plaintext message:

- Write out the complete plaintext message. Use slashes (/) to divide
  the plaintext message into recognizable words.

————— ————— ————— ————— —————

————— ————— ————— —————

Cleartext message:

- What does the coded message say?

49

Code: Date Shift code
Key: OCTOBER 31, 1994 / written **103194**

Coded message:

MEWTB LPOWU QICRH FIIQQ

Alphabet for decoding:

A B C D E F G H I J K L M N O P Q R S T U V W X Y Z

Plaintext message:

_ _ _ _ _   _ _ _ _ _   _ _ _ _ _   _ _ _ _ _

Cleartext message:

Code: Date Shift code
Key: DECEMBER 25, 1993

Coded message:

KCEPK HOKOG UHBPF OJFLD GHJUF HWQHT

Alphabet for decoding:

A B C D E F G H I J K L M N O P Q R S T U V W X Y Z

Plaintext message:

_ _ _ _ _   _ _ _ _ _   _ _ _ _ _

_ _ _ _ _   _ _ _ _ _   _ _ _ _ _

Cleartext message:

51

SECRET MESSAGE NO. 39

Code: Date Shift code
Key: JULY 4, 1776

Coded message:

BLGKH XSZHS BRDUO XIKCO OSZKR ZDIMM

Alphabet for decoding:

A B C D E F G H I J K L M N O P Q R S T U V W X Y Z

Plaintext message:

_ _ _ _ _   _ _ _ _ _   _ _ _ _ _

_ _ _ _ _   _ _ _ _ _   _ _ _ _ _

Cleartext message:

SECRET MESSAGE No. 40

Code: Date Shift code
Key: RANDOM NUMBER = **123456**

Coded message:

BHRSQ GOFKM XSPPH CFXFU RSSVB TWIID

Alphabet for decoding:

A B C D E F G H I J K L M N O P Q R S T U V W X Y Z

Plaintext message:

_ _ _ _ _   _ _ _ _ _   _ _ _ _ _   _ _ _ _ _

_ _ _ _ _   _ _ _ _ _

Cleartext message:

SECRET MESSAGE NO. 41

Code: Date Shift code
Key: RANDOM NUMBER = **987654**

Coded message:

JTSYK   ERZPT   QSEMH   TIAJZ

Alphabet for decoding:

A B C D E F G H I J K L M N O P Q R S T U V W X Y Z

Plaintext message:

_ _ _ _ _   _ _ _ _ _   _ _ _ _ _   _ _ _ _ _

Cleartext message:

SECRET MESSAGE NO. 42

Code: Date Shift code
Key: RANDOM NUMBER = **2435**

Coded message:

JEVYG QDPGW ZFUXH

Alphabet for decoding:

A B C D E F G H I J K L M N O P Q R S T U V W X Y Z

Plaintext message:

_ _ _ _ _   _ _ _ _ _   _ _ _ _ _

Cleartext message:

SECRET MESSAGE NO. 43

Code: Date Shift code
Key: RANDOM NUMBER = **252423222120**

Coded message:

INXIO HNKDF TTATT

KKYGO GEGAV

MSQTA

Alphabet for decoding:

A B C D E F G H I J K L M N O P Q R S T U V W X Y Z

Plaintext message:

————— ————— —————

————— —————

—————

Cleartext message:

56

Make Your Own Secret Message

Reverse the process you just learned!

STEP ONE: **Write your secret message:** "This is a code exercise"
Choose a code key: December 3, 1996 ("12/3/96"), written
120396

STEP TWO: Write out your message in capital letters. Give it room!
Then write the code numbers *under* the message—**one
number for each letter**—now with a little "**plus**" sign ("+")
next to it. When you run out of numbers, start over again.

T H I S   I S   A   C O D E   E X E R C I S E
+1 +2 +0 +3   +9 +6   +1   +2 +0 +3 +9   +6 +1 +2 +0 +3 +9 +6 +1

STEP THREE: Print an alphabet on a work sheet. Refer to it constantly
to save time and avoid confusion!

A B C D E F G H I J K L M N O P Q R S T U V W X Z Y

STEP FOUR:
• Look at the **first** letter of your plain English message.
It is a "T" with a "+1" underneath it.
In the alphabet above, what is "T" <u>plus one</u> letter?
It is "U."   **U is the first letter of the encoded message.**

• Look at the **second** letter of your message.
It is an "H" with a "+2" underneath it.
In the alphabet above, what is "H" <u>plus two</u> letters?
It is "J."   **J is the second letter of the encoded message.**

• Look at the **third** letter of your message.
It is an "I" with a "+0" underneath it.
In the alphabet above, what is "I" <u>plus no</u> letters?
It is still "I."   **I is the third letter of the encoded message.**

• Look at the **fourth** letter of your message.
It is an "S" with a "+3" underneath it.
In the alphabet above, what is "S" <u>plus three</u> letters?
It is "V."   **V is the fourth letter of the encoded message.**

STEP FIVE: **Write out your encoded message in five-letter groups:**

UJIVR YBEOG NKYGR FRYFX

(The final "X" is a null)

Twisted Path Code

Imagine—one dark night—that there's a knock at the window . . .
and a strange hand slips this mysterious message into your room:

After a few seconds, you'd surely make out the words . . .

SECRET MEETING AT FIVE OCLOCK

. . . in this square block of letters.

But suppose the message was . . .

CFITS LINME OVGEC CEAER KOTTE

Would you know what it means?!

Believe it or not, these cryptic 5-letter groups are in that same square
block of letters! Try to find them right now by reading each column from
bottom to top ⬆   and from **left to right** (L/R).

*

• A "twisted path" code can twist and turn any which way you like
. . . from left to right (**L/R**) . . . right to left (**R/L**) . . . top to bottom
(**T/B**) . . . or bottom to top (**B/T**). *But each time you change the path,
you also change the sequence of letters in your encoded message!*

• Here are three different encoded messages . . . all for *exactly* the
same words shown above . . . all found in the *same* 5x5 square . . .
but each one with its own "twisted path." (Follow the arrows and the
direction sign to find out which way each path goes.)

**STIFC EMNIL CEGVO
REAEC ETTOK**

⬇⬇⬇⬇⬇ L/R

**KOTTE REAEC OVGEC
EMNIL CFITS**

⬆⬇⬆⬇⬆ R/L

**ERCES TEEMT INGAT
OEVIF KCOLC**

⬅➡⬅➡ T/B

58

That 5x5 square for our **"SECRET MEETING"** message is only one kind of "matrix" (or "grid") you can use to encode a "twisted path" message. You can use different shapes and sizes, *depending on the number of "cells" in your message* (cells = message letters + any nulls you may need to fill out a short 5-letter group).

- How about a **4x5 vertical** layout for a 20-cell matrix?

S	E	N	D	
H	E	L	P	
I	M	M	E	
D	I	A	T	
E	L	Y	X	

- Or this **5x7 horizontal** layout for a 35-cell matrix?

S	O	M	E	O	N	E
H	A	S	I	N	T	E
R	C	E	P	T	E	D
O	U	R	L	A	S	T
M	E	S	S	A	G	E

!!! *Important* !!!
A "CODE KEY" MUST BE PART OF EVERY MESSAGE—
AND BOTH THE SENDER AND THE RECEIVER MUST KNOW IT!

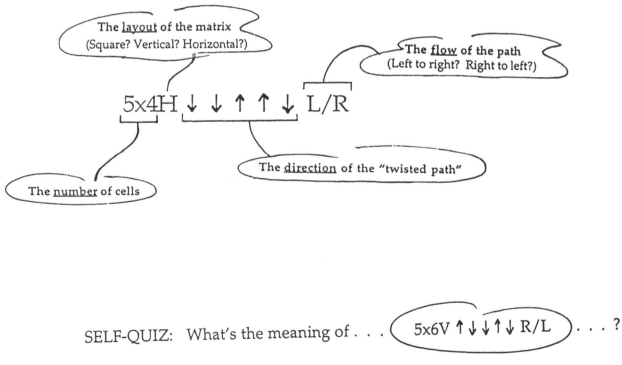

The <u>layout</u> of the matrix (Square? Vertical? Horizontal?)

The <u>flow</u> of the path (Left to right? Right to left?)

5x4H ↓ ↓ ↑ ↑ ↓ L/R

The <u>direction</u> of the "twisted path"

The <u>number</u> of cells

SELF-QUIZ: What's the meaning of . . . 5x6V ↑↓↓↑↓ R/L . . . ?

a 30-cell vertical matrix with the "twisted path" (as shown) running right-to-left

59

SECRET MESSAGE NO. 44

Code: Twisted Path code

Key: 5x5S ↑ ↓ ↑ ↓ ↑ R/L

[Reminder: This means "Draw a **square** matrix that measures **5** cells x **5** cells. Print out the coded message by following the **direction** of the 'twisted path' as shown by the arrows. In this case, the path **flows from the right side** of the matrix **to the left side**."]

Coded message:

RELNT TAERV QTNGE EEOST EMGHM

Cleartext message:

SECRET MESSAGE NO. 45

Code: Twisted Path code

Key: **10x7H** 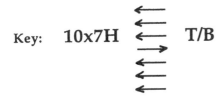 **T/B**

[Reminder: This means "Draw a **horizontal** matrix that measures **10** cells wide x **7** cells high. Print out the coded message by following the **direction** of the 'twisted path' as shown by the arrows. In this case, the path **flows from the top** of the matrix **to the bottom.**"]

Coded message:

YLLAU TNEVE SSELD RAGER ESNOC EHTFO QUENC ESWEW

MOTEV AHLLI UCSID OTTEE SMRET ENTSS

Cleartext message:

61

SECRET MESSAGE NO. 46

Code: Twisted Path code

Key: 4x5V ↓ ↑ ↓ ↑ R/L

[Reminder: "V" describes a **vertical** matrix. Otherwise, follow the usual instructions.]

Coded message:

YBFWP EOOED DLRLE KAPIU

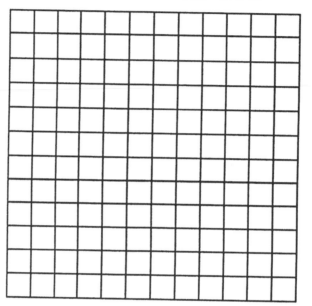

Cleartext message:

SECRET MESSAGE NO. 47

Code: Twisted Path code

Key: **9x5H**   ⟵
                      ⟵   **B/T**   [Which way does this path flow?]
                      ⟵
                      ⟵
                      ⟵

Coded message:

RDEBN IYATS REHTA RDITU
BOGIK ROWOT FFOST IOHIH OHIHR

Cleartext message:

SECRET MESSAGE NO. 48

Code: Twisted Path code

Key: 5x5S ↑ ↑ ↓ ↑ ↑ R/L

Coded message:

ROEMF VLLET NCNEE SMINO OTEED

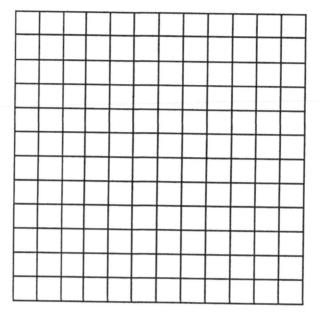

Cleartext message:

SECRET MESSAGE NO. 49

Code: Twisted Path code

Key: 7x5V ↑ ↓ ↑ ↓ ↑ L/R

Coded message:

TMHWA ICRNS NEIRE
LOBYI UISDY LLAMS DTOES

Cleartext message:

SECRET MESSAGE No. 50

Code: Twisted Path code

Key: 10x4V ↓ ↓ ↓ ↑ L/R

Coded message:

NNHNR DGIOG OSIOO AOTRX
RNTER SSSIM GNBHH SRSOU

Cleartext message:

SECRET MESSAGE NO. 51

Code: Twisted Path code

Key: **9x10V** ↓ ↑ ↑ ↓ ↑ ↑ ↓ ↓ ↑ **L/R**

Coded message:

TEIZO HJRAO UNYOO
TINNH RCPYP STEDI SOFSO
EETEB UXODY FBOFI DTAOO FERTS
THNEU UULED HEONN ERLNY WFICN YLWLE

[Watch out for a new twist with the nulls!]

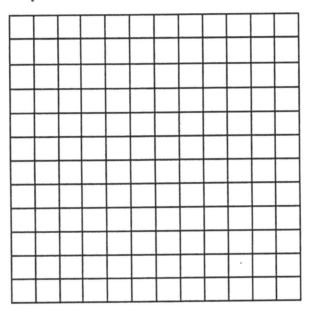

Cleartext message:

67

Make Your Own Secret Message

Reverse the decoding process when you want to encode your own message to dispatch to your fellow cryptographer. Here's how to do it.

STEP ONE: Write your secret message. This is *our* message for today:

ARE YOU READY TO DO SOME HEAVY-DUTY CRYPTOGRAPHY? I AM!

STEP TWO   Count the number of letters in the message. Don't count punctuation.
There are **43** letters in our message.

STEP THREE: Do you need nulls to fill out the message? (The message has to divide evenly into 5-letter groups.)
Our message needs **2** nulls to even out to 45 "cells."
We've picked the nulls **XZ**.

STEP FOUR: Choose a matrix with enough cells to fit the message.
There are two possibilities for a 45-cell message: a 9x5 horizontal matrix or a 5x9 vertical matrix.
Let's go with **9x5H**.

STEP FIVE: Outline that matrix on a piece of grid paper. Then write in the message.

A	R	E	Y	O	U	R	E	A
D	Y	T	O	D	O	S	O	M
E	H	E	A	V	Y	D	U	T
Y	C	R	Y	P	T	O	G	R
A	P	H	Y	I	A	M	X	Z

STEP SIX: Make up a "twisted path." Here's ours: ↑ ↑ ↓ ↓ ↑ ↓ ↓ ↑ ↑ L/R

Use that "twisted path" to encode the message . . .

**AYEDA PCHYR ETERH YOAYY
IPVDO UOYTA RSDOM
XGUOE ZRTMA**

STEP SEVEN: Send that secret message to your fellow codebreaker . . .
. . . BUT DON'T FORGET TO INCLUDE THE CODE KEY!

Our code key is: | 9x5H ↑ ↑ ↓ ↓ ↑ ↓ ↓ ↑ ↑   L/R |

Solutions
to the
Secret Messages

Solutions to the Secret Messages

(NULLS appear as capital letters in parentheses.)

SIMPLE LETTER GROUPING

Secret Message No. 1 / page 4
Patience and Fortitude are renown landmarks, and the "mane" guardians, at the main entrance of the New York Public Library located at Fifth Avenue and Forty-second Street in New York City, AKA [also known as] "The Big Apple." (OQBR)

Secret Message No. 2 / page 5
"The Lone Eagle"—Charles Augustus Lindbergh—flew "The Spirit of St. Louis" on his historic flight, which in retrospect can be likened to the placing of the first span of the now much-traveled "air bridge." (RWMB)

Secret Message No. 3 / page 6
The profusion of products related to the inventive genius of Thomas Alva Edison touch the lives of the majority of the population spanning the globe, contributing to their comfort and well-being. (BCR)

Secret Message No. 4 / page 7
Exhibiting rare foresight, blessed with oratorical magnificence and possessing aspirations and dreams beyond compare, Dr. Martin Luther King Jr. was a singular giant with the power of outstanding leadership. (Q)

Secret Message No. 5 / page 8
Creator and conductor of the "underground railroad," the astonishing innovator Harriet Tubman, though born a slave, held forth a free spirit, exhibited feats of remarkable heroism and became an inspiration to peoples of the free world. (TZ)

Secret Message No. 6 / page 9
Recognized for her distinguished career as an assistant attorney general, state senator and a Superior Court judge, Sandra Day O'Conner, born in El Paso, TX, was the first woman appointed to serve as an associate justice of the U. S. Supreme Court. (MZ)

Secret Message No. 7 / page 10
Notable among American jurists, Ruth Bader Ginsberg, born in Brooklyn, NY, is the second woman appointed to the Supreme Court. A professor of law, she gained wide recognition and was noted for her accomplishments toward helping to end institutionalized discrimination against women. (X)

Secret Message No. 8 / page 11
(PTRP) Nurturing the Theory of Relativity, Albert Einstein became a Nobel Laureate for his work in physics. Although some of his concepts and theories did not gain universal acceptance, his scientific and social efforts and free thinking gained him worldwide recognition.

THE REVERSE TRAIL

Secret Message No. 9 / page 14 — Thanks for nothing. (EOES)
Secret Message No. 10 / page 15 — Jack be nimble, Jack be quick before you get stuck in a rut. (MQRV)
Secret Message No. 11 / page 16 — All's well that ends well.
Secret Message No. 12 / page 17 — The first shall be last and the last shall be first. (MTRT)
Secret Message No. 13 / page 18 — Let's make hay while the sun shines. (MW)
Secret Message No. 14 / page 19 — A bird in the hand is worth two in the bush. (RV)
Secret Message No. 15 / page 20 — You can never have too much of a good thing. (O)
Secret Message No. 16 / page 21 — Better a half a loaf than no bread at all. (RXO)

SHIFT CODE

KEY WORD CODE

DATE SHIFT CODE

TWISTED PATH CODE